FSC
www.fsc.org
MIX
Papier aus ver-
antwortungsvollen
Quellen
Paper from
responsible sources
FSC® C105338

AF306864

Bibliographic information of the German National Library:
The German National Library lists this publication in the German
National Bibliography; detailed bibliographic data is available
on the Internet at dnb.dnb.de.

© 2024 Regina Toedter Translated from the German
with the original title "Alkohol-Killer. Die 50 besten Tipps"
("Alcohol killer. The 50 best tips").
Herstellung und Verlag: BoD – Books on Demand, Norderstedt

2015 Original edition published by Trias Verlag Stuttgart by MVS
Medizinverlage Stuttgart (Germany). 2nd edition reprinted in 2019 by
Goldmann Verlag by Random House Munich (Germany).

ISBN: 9783758368929

Alcohol-free. The 50 best tips

by Regina Toedter

About the book

A cold beer to cool down, a glass of red wine to relax - for many people this is quite normal. Drinking alcohol is an integral part of our culture. We drink because it tastes good and because (almost) everyone does it. However, we all too easily forget that even 0.3 per mille can lead to alcohol intoxication and have health consequences. Regina Toedter shows how easy it can be to consciously say no to alcohol with **Alkohol-free. The 50 best tips**. It helps you to question your own drinking behaviour and provides a self-test for your individual status quo. Because being "alcohol-free" means feeling better and fitter, looking fresher and healthier, being more flexible and more alert.

About the author

After studying cultural sciences at university and training as a fitness and running coach, **Regina Toedter** now works as a communications manager and health author. In search of writing inspiration, she used to reach for a glass of wine herself from time to time. At the age of 28, she made a conscious decision to give up alcohol for a week - that was 11 years ago, and she still doesn't miss it.

More books by the author

Die 50 besten Zuckersucht-Killer
("The 50 best sugar addiction killers") (TRIAS)

Machs einfach! ("Just do it!") (TRIAS)

Buddha räumt auf ("Buddha tidies up") (südwest)

Der Glückscoach – Entschleunigen
("The happiness coach – slow down") (TRIAS)

You can also read Regina Toedter's health column in
FOCUS magazine

Regina Toedter

Alcohol-free

The 50 best tips

Content

Preface instead of preheating

Dear readers, let's be honest...

If we think about it more carefully, we should be sceptical: We've been drinking something for years that we don't need either physically or mentally. Quite the opposite. It makes us tired, sometimes dizzy and clouds our minds. We are talking about alcohol (or ethanol, as the correct chemical name is). Alcohol robs us of our energy for the next day and generally just makes us feel dull and drained the next morning. In the worst case, we can't even remember the night before. But the gossip in the office has already done the rounds. Oh dear, it was supposed to be just one drink. Now we've got a stupid flirt on our hands, misplaced our great cardigan and the mountain of tasks is still there and has to be tackled with a headache. Why do we drink alcohol at all when we know that we often regret it the next morning? Why is it so difficult to give up and how can we reduce our own consumption? These are three basic questions - and they are all wrong.

We don't actually have to answer the WHY. That's more a job for doctors and psychologists. All we know is that we drink it because everyone does it somehow, sometimes it simply does us good after a particularly bad day and lightens the mood. Alcohol is an integral part of our culture, has a long tradition and accompanies us at every turn. Hardly anyone can imagine dancing "sober" at their next wedding, can they?

The second question turns out to be a cultural misconception, because we don't actually have to give it up. Alcohol is not essential to life - it is an additive, a stimulant, an emotional enhancer and inhibitor that we find difficult to control once the first glass has been downed. For many people, alcohol often serves as a substitute for a possibly unsatisfactory situation or an unfulfilled desire, doesn't it? So we need to rethink: if we stop drinking alcohol in future, then please do so consciously, voluntarily and intentionally. There are many liquid alternatives that, unlike alcohol, are actually beneficial to our health and enrich our everyday lives. These naturally include water, tea, juices and spritzers. But it goes beyond the drink: we need new rituals, options and creative ideas - alcohol-free ones, of course.

And the question of reduction includes the question of the right measure. But who determines the scale of values? Isn't this a very individual question? And don't most people only cut back when they notice something wrong with their health? But when your health starts to go on strike, isn't it almost too late?

So let's ask ourselves how and with what tricks we can cheat alcohol and what advantages there are in giving up alcohol. After all, we encounter alcohol every day anyway. A glass is held under our noses at almost every party, at the weekend and even in everyday life.

But we don't need alcohol all the time! Just think about it: alcohol-free means feeling better and fitter. You also look fresher, younger and healthier. You can use your alcohol-free days (and evenings) longer, more profoundly and more intensively without alcohol. Of course, because you are 100% there! Lows - which are a normal part of life - but also creative holes, unpleasant moments, boring evenings, frustration and crisis situations can also be dealt with successfully when sober. Life has many little moments of happiness in store, but you have to be alert to them. In a tipsy state, you will at most stumble across such opportunities, but not realise them. Alcohol basically has only one purpose: it provides a brief firework display in your head, but then clouds your vision in the long term. In addition, we often feel tired, groggy and desolate after a short time. In the long term, regular alcohol consumption can also make us seriously ill.

That's great! So let's get rid of it! Alcohol doesn't deliver what it promises. How could it? Behind its perfect image is an industry worth billions that knows exactly what it's doing. Alcohol makes some people addicted quite quickly (because we love this short kick, it's readily available, cheap and immediately effective).

But we have a free choice. Saying no to alcohol makes us independent, more flexible, more mindful and free. However, this does not automatically mean that we have to give up future celebrations and parties, nor does it mean that we have to give up enjoyment or fun.

On the contrary! Happiness, cheerfulness and joy begin in the mind, not in the drip! Flick the switch - and let yourself be inspired and surprised by the 50 best tips for an "alcohol-free" life from now on.

Have fun and success,
Regina Toedter

Little helpers

The main question now is how to really get alcohol out of sight. Is this even possible - what does it look like in practice?

We encounter alcohol every day. That's the first challenge. Find out the basics about everyday life in the first part of the book. Take the quick test and spontaneously take a break from alcohol. Rethink your previous (drinking) locations and friends. Perhaps you will reshuffle the cards here and venture into new encounters.

Sobering situations: The second challenge - which we face every day - are those typical occasions that tempt us to drink: the nice barbecue in summer, the next colourful birthday party, the annual Christmas party, New Year, milestone anniversaries, the long-awaited holiday, the occasional party night or the usual visit to our favourite restaurant. How do you cope with such situations when you are trying not to drink? Have you ever tried to flirt sober? Imagine you can do it and maybe you'll finally fall in love! This might save you a nasty surprise the next day when you can't remember anyone's name or don't know exactly what you talked about on your first date. Learn the best tricks in this chapter to stay happy and dry in social gatherings.

Simply saying "no" to alcohol more often has many positive effects. One of them is, of course, your health. Read in the "Salute" section about the great benefits of giving up alcohol. Not only will you sleep better, but you will also save yourself the scary picture in front of the mirror the next morning. You can also find out what else you can save yourself in this chapter.

Change your bad habits (such as frequent alcohol consumption) and put your good intentions into practice. You can find inspiration in the following chapter on habits - and if necessary, ask the experts mentioned there. Did you know that you are already a trendsetter with your alcohol reduction plan? You can finally enjoy long weekends without alcohol, how? Find out in this chapter!

And when the next party comes round, you'll have plenty of fruity-fresh friends at the start who you can sip until you drop. You can find the recipes in the "Non-alcoholic drinks" chapter. Your guests will be amazed. Or do you know what the green stuff in your glass is?

If you do fall into the alcohol trap again and have had a bit too much to drink, there's no need to worry. Now you need a few handy hangover tips. Debunk misleading myths, go on a Kneipp tour and then "slip into your boots". I'll show you why in the last chapter! If you're still swaying back and forth, take the "alcohol test" right away.

I hope you enjoy reading and putting the 50 best tips for an "alcohol-free" everyday life into practice: No alcohol is also a solution, and with this in mind: "Prosit" (Latin for "May it be useful")!

Al(c)day

In which situations do you reach for alcoholic drinks? Never seriously thought about it? Then do it now.

Think about it: Why do you drink alcohol at all? How long has it been part of your everyday life and how would it feel to give it up (consciously and voluntarily)? The first tips below will give you some food for thought.

1 Quick test: an alcohol-free week

Let's move on to the $1 million question: "Do you drink too much alcohol?!" Let's ask the audience: Are your loved ones calling you a "social drinker" or even a "booze hound" again? Hm, that doesn't mean anything, you think! Take a look back at the past week: There was the barbecue party at Peters' at the weekend, there were sausages, salad and of course the beer was not to be missed. On Monday morning, we toasted our 10th anniversary with champagne at work and Tuesdays are always girls' night. This time we went to the cinema and the glass of Prosecco was free! On Wednesday, we unfortunately had to resort to bitters, which always helps so well with digestive problems. And on Thursday, the spouse opened the good red wine for dinner after the children had gone to bed on time. Of course, Fridays are always the start of the weekend, and this time we went to the city festival, including happy hour in our favourite bar.

Have you noticed anything now? Perhaps you've also noticed yourself that it's become a bit more lately. No problem, because you can cut down at any time. Take the quick test now and take an alcohol-free break. Observe how easy or difficult it is for you not to drink for a week (or longer). And the great thing is: you're holding lots of jokers in your hands right now, namely 50 great tips for an alcohol-free everyday life, doesn't that sound like a jackpot? Here we go.

2 Fight boredom!

The consumption of alcohol is often linked to boredom. How is that? Although we are constantly busy and always on the go, rarely have time and seem to have a thousand things to do, an inner emptiness often emerges and the question of meaning arises. But because work and daily commitments fill our everyday lives to such an extent, hobbies, social relationships and animalistic conversations often fall by the wayside. We may become more superficial and passive, as evidenced by our thoughtless participation in parties and celebrations where we like to drink to excess, which we rarely question. We also often find boredom unpleasant. Very few of us can stand peace, silence and doing nothing. We look for immediate distraction, at best combined with immediate feelings of happiness.

Good thing we have this "alcohol" option: We can experience, get high, feel numb and happy to a certain extent - after just a few sips. Alcohol, that perfect mood booster, isn't it? But what if we gradually learn to accept boredom as a normal part of life and, at best, use it creatively?

Let's try a change of perspective and a thought experiment: doing nothing as a creative break, as (self-)reflection and a stopping point. This also slows down our busy schedules and we may come across wishes and ideas that we have long since drowned. Don't fight the inner emptiness with high spirits, but with the gradual realisation of your true interests.

3 Avoid favourite pubs and drinking buddies

Everyone has them and everyone loves them in some way: the nice drinking friends with whom you meet up for a relaxed beer at the weekend - or rather two, three or four? After all, someone is always throwing a round. Not exactly conducive if you want to reduce your consumption. So instead of meeting up at the cocktail bar on Saturdays as usual, go out for brunch with your friends on Sunday mornings instead (just swap the welcome champagne for an extra cup of cappuccino).

Do you have friends and mates with whom you only have a "drinking friendship"? You can find out very quickly by telling them about your alcohol-free plan and waiting for their reaction. If they just make silly comments or don't take you seriously, then you know. However, if they show you serious interest, take these genuine friends on board and talk openly and honestly about your plans. It's important that you don't have to double-track or pretend. Take a close look at your everyday situations: the occasional visit to the neighbour's house, where not only coffee but also champagne is served, as well as the new position of responsibility in your company, which turns out to be a catalyst for frequent frustration drinking after work. Question the motivation for your drinking behaviour and take the reins into your own hands.

4 Strengthen your safety net

Intuitively, people withdraw when they are overwhelmed by a difficult situation and are threatened with failure. The stigma of failure is too great in a meritocracy like ours. We don't want to make a mountain out of a molehill, right? And suddenly a situation seems hopeless! You then have qualms about bragging about not drinking alcohol and having to admit failure later. It's at times like this that you need a good friend to keep you going. We depend on each other, and that's a good thing! Talking is balm for the soul and helps to clear the mind! So tell your loved ones, and it also helps at parties when hosts and guests know that you are just sitting there and not constantly making tempting offers.

By sharing and reflecting with like-minded people, we can find solutions that we cannot find on our own. But rather than sitting at home waiting for a friendly phone call, we should, to paraphrase Gandhi, be the friend we want to be. This requires initiative. We should always work on our social relationships, as psychologists also emphasise, if we want our lives to be as happy and successful as possible. Take advantage of the current situation of change and reconsider individual "drinking friendships". Make new ones too. And maybe one or two of your drinking friends will spontaneously jump on the bandwagon and you can brave the alcohol together. It's easier, and you can turn peer pressure on its head, making the drinker the bogeyman. It definitely works better together.

Part of a good friendship is talking openly about alcohol. Do you feel that some of the friends you spend a lot of time with are drinking a little too much? And over a long period of time? Do you know why? No matter how strong your friendship is, it is still a sensitive topic and should be approached with caution.

Unfortunately, the subject is often presented as harmless or even taboo, or people quickly feel offended. After all, you don't want to tread on anyone's toes, and you certainly don't want to make a bad judgement. Nevertheless, it is important to show your friend that you are concerned and that you can be trusted. There are also many helplines (more on this later) where you can get help. The only thing you can really do wrong is to ignore the situation and keep quiet.

5 Thirst for knowledge instead of drinking

To be honest, if you look at the subject of alcohol and its consequences, you will literally lose your thirst! Just googling the term "drunk" can take away any desire to drink, and the photos and videos shown are actually quite embarrassing. Nevertheless, we should approach the subject seriously and sensitively and take a look behind the scenes.

Another aspect is the seriously increasing problem of alcoholism, which is not just the sad picture on our streets. Alcohol abuse and addiction are problems that are often recognised too late and can affect anyone, at any age, in any society.

By exchanging ideas with others and gaining knowledge on the subject, you can start doing some basic prevention and awareness-raising work for yourself and those around you. Broaden your horizons, because you can never learn enough. For example, expose common advertising lies and demythologise the supposed positive effects of alcoholic drinks. Advertising typically uses positive attribution patterns that people like to identify with and apply to their own lives. Beer, for example, promises freedom, freshness, purity and enjoyment; sparkling wine alludes to passion, excitement, exclusivity and wealth; rum promises a paradisiacal, carefree lifestyle with rhythmic sounds and sunshine; and vodka, with its "pure soul", guarantees freshness, fun and clarity. The more you study the subject, the more you will become aware of the problem. In the future, simply replace the desire to drink with a thirst for knowledge.

6 Give yourself a kick, without alcohol

Getting high without alcohol sounds like an illegal substance, don't you think? But don't panic. The opiates we're talking about here are completely natural and absolutely harmless. You carry them around with you practically every day. We're talking about dopamine, serotonin, endorphins and adrenaline. These are the body's own happiness hormones that ensure your personal well-being, confidence, balance, but also stimulation and euphoria. All you need to do is "activate" these endogenous happiness hormones. The best way to do this is through sufficient exercise, enough daylight, fresh air and a positive attitude.

Think "good" and generate the power of happiness from within. You can also help, for example, with happy food, i.e. certain foods such as cocoa, dates, bananas or nuts. Real mood killers, on the other hand, are fast food products that make us listless or even depressed. Also be careful with chocolate. It is not the sugar it contains, but the tryptophan in cocoa that makes us high. It is therefore better to choose dark chocolate rather than milk chocolate with a high sugar content. The mere sight of chocolate makes us so excited that dopamine is released in the brain.

Extratip

Depending on your preference and physical condition, an action film, a ride on the chain carousel or a blind date can provide an intense hormone release. Or you can jump from the 3-metre board in the outdoor pool, give a speech in front of an audience, climb a high tower, run a marathon, take an ice-cold shower, look out of the window when there's thunder and lightning or really step on the gas on the motorway. Whatever gives you a kick - do it!

Rely on your personal happiness centre and look forward to exhilarating moments.

7 Set drinking days

Let's be honest, it's always difficult to find the right balance. Once you've washed down one glass, the barriers fall and the desire for more is ignited. How much is "enough" is a matter of debate. In any case, we all know that good intentions can't always be kept (and certainly not when you're already tipsy). A dilemma! In theory, the easiest thing to do would probably be to give it a miss altogether. But you don't have to go to extremes. So perhaps try having fixed drinking days. Think very carefully about when and how much alcohol is appropriate for you. Should it only be a glass of sparkling wine for your birthday, New Year's Eve or milestone anniversaries? Do you only want to open a glass of wine at the weekend with a meal, or do you only treat yourself to a cool beer or two on holiday?

Once you have defined a healthy amount for yourself, commit to it and get down to business. If you find yourself repeatedly throwing your drinking plan overboard and drinking significantly more than planned, you should seriously consider the cause! As the saying goes, the exception proves the rule, but the exception should not become the rule. In other words: sometimes complete abstinence helps to avoid temptation in the first place.

8 Goofy – don´t be silly!

Last year (2023), the word "goofy" was chosen as the most popular word among young people. Based on the famous cartoon character from Walt Disney, the word refers to a clumsy, stupid person who others can only laugh at. Even those who drink to excess can quickly be described as "goofy" due to their silly and sometimes embarrassing behaviour when drunk (nothing to be proud of).

Being silly is not a bad thing in itself. Silly people have a positive attitude, they are playful, usually have a great sense of humour and like to laugh or make others laugh.

However, if these positive characteristics are the result of alcohol consumption, alarm bells should ring. Silliness as a result of excessive drinking can lead to embarrassing or inappropriate behaviour, which can result in social stigma or embarrassment. When drunk, situations can no longer be properly assessed. This disrupts interpersonal relationships and leads to misunderstandings, conflicts and rash decisions.

Don't be a "goofy" person who constantly puts his foot in his mouth, but remain professional and authentic. Of course, you can be funny sometimes, do nonsensical things and have a good time. But you don't need alcohol to enjoy life with a smile on your face, that's for sure! There are many ways to have a happy and fulfilling life and stay healthy at the same time. Let this reading inspire you to try some of them.

Sober situations

A barbecue without beer? An evening with friends without a glass of wine or a cocktail? Is that even possible?

Wow! It's amazing how omnipresent alcohol actually is. In this chapter, we take a closer look and ask ourselves what normal situations that we associate with alcohol (in a restaurant, on a night out, when flirting or at a barbecue) might look like if we really gave up alcoholic drinks. Won't this make us an outsider, will we have to justify ourselves every time, play the chauffeur or listen to what a party pooper we are? Not necessarily! After all, you can also toast with mineral water and the fun factor shouldn't depend on the alcohol level. It shouldn't come to that! Because if you've now gathered enough thought-provoking, interesting background information and have developed an appetite for an alcohol-free life, you'll take a more relaxed approach from now on: For inspiration, read on to find out what this can look like in a playful way, what standard phrases you should adopt and where it's better to keep quiet.

9 Find your flow

After a particularly exhausting day at work, we look forward to our well-deserved evening off the most. This is sacred to us and we don't usually have much time for it. That's why we naturally want to make the most of these few hours. The perfect transition can be ritualised: A delicious dinner with the family, a hot shower and the evening news. For many people, a glass of red wine, a cold beer or a nightcap is a must. But before we know it, the alcoholic drink has become an integral part of our leisure activities and our evening ritual and it's hard to imagine life without it.

Instead of getting drunk, it's better to be independent and "downshift" naturally: It's all about balance, and the best way to switch off is with an activity that really gets you into the flow. The term comes from psychology and describes a state of being completely absorbed in an activity in which you forget everything around you. The source of flow can be very different: For some it is creative work, for others an exciting book, a walk in the woods or strumming a guitar. A hobby with flow does not require alcoholic support. Find your personal passion and make time for it in the evening. Enjoy the evening not with alcohol, but with peace and relaxation to recharge your batteries.

10 Toast to your health

Cheerful exclamations such as "Chin-chin", "Skâl", "Kanpai", "Prost", "Na sdorowje", "Cheers", "Salute" and similar are part of an intercultural custom that can be found almost everywhere in the world. Toasting each other seems to be universal and brings the most diverse people together. It overcomes barriers, creates friendships and emphasises the reason for being together. To toast means to be welcome, to drink to love, to a happy future, to health and to oneself. It is not uncommon for a short speech to be made while the glass is raised. Then the contents end up in the stomach and sometimes the glasses fly against the wall.

The exact origin of the custom of raising a toast is difficult to understand today. It is said to "drive away evil spirits", which make themselves felt the next morning with a hangover. But why drive the spirits away if you don't call them in the first place (no alcohol = no hangover)? And what evil spirits are we actually talking about here? They have no place in a party. Put an end to the spook! You can also toast with non-alcoholic drinks, for example lemonade, fruit spritzers or non-alcoholic sparkling wine. Because when toasting, it is the congratulations that matter and not the alcohol content in the glass. If you think about it, toasting your health with alcohol makes no sense. You drink to your health and paradoxically do the opposite. So, be a great role model and set a good example.

11 Don't be thirsty anymore

A cosy evening with friends, the last warm sunrays tickle your skin and the smell of a sausage or vegetable kebab fills your nose. You're thirsty and thinking about a cold beer for refreshment? Bad idea! Unfortunately, alcohol doesn't quench your thirst. On the contrary: alcohol draws even more fluids from the body, which makes itself felt after a few hours through discomfort and headaches. If you're having a barbecue, it's better to mix up some tasty, fruity and delicious vitamin bombs. A fruit punch or a sparkling juice bowl are perfect cool-down drinks (more on this later). If you don't have ice cubes to hand, you can also try lukewarm tea for a change.

Because our bodies are actually quite sensitive to cold drinks! We have to "adapt" the liquid to our body temperature. This in turn requires even more physical energy and actually only results in more sweating. It is not without reason that hot tea is served in particularly hot countries (e.g. Egypt or Morocco): It relieves the body, cools and quenches thirst. With a little peppermint or a pinch of cinnamon, you can also give your barbecue an oriental flavour.

12 Eating out without drinking

We encounter alcohol almost everywhere, especially when eating out. So your next visit to a restaurant can be a bit of a test. But you are prepared and don't have to hide from your favourite Italian restaurant: let the food melt in your mouth, taste every single ingredient and concentrate fully on the lovingly prepared plate. Take your time and enjoy the ambience. Water or spritzers go wonderfully with the main course and even help you to hold back while you eat.

Make sure you bring plenty to talk about, because you know the "delaying tactics" in restaurants, which are probably designed to encourage alcohol consumption. And instead of ordering the next bottle of wine during these waiting times, talk about interesting topics and find out more about the other person. Now that you are no longer drinking alcohol with your meal, you will also pay more attention to your feeling of fullness. Goodbye stomach ache! And if you do accidentally stuff yourself with delicious food, keep your hands off the booze and combine your visit to the restaurant with a walk in the nearby park. Exercise promotes digestion in a much friendlier way than herbal schnapps (more on this in the tip "Herbal tea instead of herbal schnapps"). If the restaurant serves you a short drink "on the house" with your bill, refuse with thanks (or simply leave the glass) without being embarrassed or having to explain. No one will take offence. Perhaps you can negotiate an espresso instead. Just ask!

13 Flirt sober

Flirting is magic, do you agree? Either a miracle happens and your crush speaks to you, or you urgently need a "magic potion" for that extra dose of bravery. You can rely on alcohol: Alcohol works quickly and supposedly boosts self-esteem. We even dare to make the first move and perhaps find the right topic of conversation straight away. In reality, however, we don't become more self-confident, but in the worst case we start babbling, smelling out of our mouths, staggering and saying meaningless things. We're really in trouble the next morning when our prince might turn into a frog again - what a bad surprise!

Flirting is a highly complex matter and at least as exciting as an important job interview (where you will of course be sober, right?!): Swap the beer for an apple spritzer and give the other person your full attention. Then you'll quickly find a common topic that connects you. Talk about travelling, interests, books, sports, music tastes. These are usually always good first points of contact. With humour and sincere compliments, you will eventually break the ice. But even the occasional seemingly awkward pause should not be a problem for you, because shared silence is the perfect opportunity for eye contact with a sizzling effect. Make yourself interesting, but don't push yourself to the fore. No one wants to meet an egocentric person and certainly not a drunk one. So take courage and you'll have a happy ending!

14 Party without alcohol

Granted, the next party night can feel pretty weird sober when everyone around you is getting drunker and drunker and you end up just being the driver. But if you enjoy going dancing, it's at least as much fun when you're sober. It may take a little more effort, but without alcohol in your blood, you can feel the music better and also enjoy your athletic endurance (more on this in the section "Dance yourself into a trance"). If you drink less alcohol or none at all, you can also leave the party before everyone else is overly drunk. The advantage of this is that you are well-rested and fit the next day. After such an alcohol-free night, you only realise how superficial some evenings can become the later it gets and the drunker the people are. At some point, it's almost impossible to have a good conversation and unfortunately, as a "sober" person, you're often just a shrink or even a buzzkill. But let's take it sporty: you can still have fun.

It depends on your point of view. What is your attitude to life? After all, humour is a way of life and cannot be measured in per mille. Look for friends who also don't drink and suggest other leisure activities (e.g. going to the cinema or outdoor pool, attending a reading, cooking together, climbing or going on a city trip). Real friends will come along and who knows, maybe they will also enjoy drinking without alcohol.

Be careful not to tell everyone about your abstinence at a party where there is a lot of drinking. This can be provocative for others. Don't get involved in discussions with drunks and avoid attempts to explain and justify yourself. This is pointless. Either you are judged as a party pooper, a good person or even "seriously ill". Many people immediately think that someone who drinks little or no alcohol must have a real alcohol problem, and then questions come up such as "Did something bad happen to you in the past?", "Do your parents drink?", "Did someone in your family die because of it?". These are questions you don't want to have to deal with in a nice company, right? So if you're at a party that you enjoy and you don't know anyone anyway, it's better to stay undercover. Honestly, no one is looking into your glass and no one really cares what you're drinking. Most people are so busy with themselves that they won't notice if you're drinking apple juice instead of beer, sparkling water instead of champagne or grape juice instead of red wine. If necessary, change the person you are talking to or use a white lie ("I have a bad headache today! ", "I have to get up early tomorrow for an important appointment" or "I'm travelling by car"). If someone suddenly offers you an alcoholic drink, simply keep it in your hand for a while and put it down at a good moment when nobody is looking. If you are suddenly "unmasked" after all, practise silence and don't be afraid to leave an assumption in the room.

16 Use your rights

Constantly looking for excuses not to drink is of course annoying! Everyone has the right to refuse something without immediately being discredited. But people don't always understand this, especially when it comes to alcohol. You can either argue endlessly, remain silent or come up with funny excuses (as you learned in the previous tip 'Stay undercover'), or you can invoke the fundamental human right enshrined in international law (for example, the European Union's Charter of Fundamental Rights, Article 10): The right to freedom of religion or belief. The phrase "I don't drink because of my religion" really defuses any potential tension and immediately keeps the peace! Questions are rare because religion and ideology are not discussed and criticism is absolutely taboo. It doesn't really matter which religion or ideology you are referring to. In particular, many Buddhists, most Muslims and some Christians live a life of total abstinence, believing that alcohol is incompatible with a spiritual orientation and a positive attitude to life. This is a valid point, so don't hesitate to use it as a reason.

17 Go on an alcohol-free holiday

Whether you're going to the sea, the mountains, planning a city trip or holidaying on a balcony - holidays are something special! On holiday, we want to relax and have lots of fun. It would be a shame if we only got to experience half of it, just sit at the pool bar and while away the days sobering up. Unfortunately, relaxation and fun are often equated with alcohol and the all-inclusive offer is utilised to the last drop.

On holiday, we can do without alcohol altogether, because we drink to calm down, lift our mood or forget the stress of everyday life. We don't need that anymore! It happens all by itself on holiday. The change of location alone takes our mind off things. Foreign cultures are both inspiring and exciting. It's fun to go on a journey of discovery, meet new people and lose track of time. Speaking of time, don't be surprised how "long" a holiday without alcohol suddenly seems. You stretch your holiday time noticeably, isn't that great? At the same time, this time is ideal for switching off from everyday life. You now have much more energy at your disposal and are really in the mood for excursions. Explore the foreign city in jogging shoes, savour the exotic cuisine and learn a new skill (language, pottery or drumming).

But be careful: especially on holiday, you will often fall into alcohol traps if you are not travelling to a Muslim country like Dubai. Plan your next trip completely alcohol-free and you will be surprised how much you will benefit from it.

18 Enjoy unforgettable evenings

And another year has passed. The birthday is approaching, New Year's Eve is just around the corner and the anniversary reaches a round number. There are certain celebrations in the year that we cannot and should not avoid. These events are far too beautiful and precious! But we can celebrate without alcohol. When we are sober, we finally realise what we are actually celebrating: The focus is finally on people, the past year with its ups and downs and the happy moment. It is not without reason that we say: "It's good that you were born" and wish each other: "Happy New Year! We should always remember this and not let alcohol be the reason we have fun. Parties without alcohol are legendary: as the host, surprise your guests with unusual drinks: fiery vitamin shots, colourful fruit cocktails, sparkling bowls or homemade smoothies (you can find more ideas in the "Alcohol-free drinks" section).

But it's not just about the drinks, convince with delicious finger food, a fun programme and good music. You're sure to have a few great feel-good songs up your sleeve that everyone will want to sing along to straight away! This in turn will help the first brave ones onto the dance floor. You can help by imitating the iconic moves of the superstars, as well as dance scenes from well-known music videos or musicals that are perfect for a successful party night. You've already learnt how to become a dancing star with zero alcohol. (take a look at the tip "Using the power of music"). Fun card games, board games and colouring games will also get the party going. Try guessing games (e.g. celebrity guessing) or theme parties (dressed up is even more fun). Poker is also almost better played sober. You can finally consciously use your poker face. Games create the desired relaxed atmosphere.

Even if the changeover to alcohol-free parties takes some getting used to at first, and some guests may say stupid things or even leave the party early, you will be surprised how much more interesting the conversations with other guests suddenly become and what exciting things you learn from your friends. And because you are consciously present with all your senses, you end up experiencing evenings that you will never forget.

Extratip

The latest scientific observations show that calcium in particular reduces the desire for alcoholic drinks. So why not reach for cheese sticks when you're out with friends in the evening or just sitting cosily in front of the TV at home. Cheese is also good for teeth and bones, regulates nerve impulses in the muscles, has an anti-inflammatory effect and has a high protein density.
But even vegans need not worry: Calcium is present not only in dairy products, but also in green vegetables and nuts - both of which are great for snacking on.

Salute to your health

Their own health is very important to many people and, paradoxically, some people like to toast to it - which is actually strange.

One of the most common reasons why people stop drinking is their health. Sometimes the doctor has to point this out to them, but then the excuses stop very quickly and it is suddenly no longer so difficult getting back to a healthier lifestyle. Drinking a toast to your own health - with alcohol to boot - really is a huge contradiction! With this chapter, you might kill two birds with one stone, because if you give up alcohol from now on, you can finally put all your good intentions (such as better health, happiness, less stress, weight loss) into practice.

19 Save it!

The beer may only cost you a few dollars and you can sometimes get a good wine on offer, but the amount adds up over the days and at the end of the month you have a few hundred dollars less in your wallet. And you know yourself that it rarely stops at one glass. Then you throw the next round and there's always a reason to celebrate. However, if you manage to put the dollar aside each time instead of buying alcoholic drinks, you can save a lot. Your health will thank you and, by the way, you'll also have saved a pretty penny that you can spend on other nice things.

A small calculation example (of course, this calculation is not compatible with all countries in the world, simply exchange the sum for your currency - you will see that it amounts to the same thing): At the weekend, you spend an average of perhaps 10 to 20 dollars on alcoholic drinks. You meet up with friends, go out to eat and order wine (5 to 10 dollars). On Sunday, the weather is fine, you have a barbecue and drink a few bottles of beer (2 to 5 dollars). It's your colleague's birthday, you toast with Prosecco (3 dollars) and during the week you meet your best friend, discuss "men's problems" and have a few glasses of cream liqueur (4 to 8 dollars). Let's take stock: on average, you spend 30 to 40 dollars a week on alcohol alone. At the end of the year, we end up with a considerable 1500 dollars. For some people, it will certainly be a few hundred euros more. Think of weddings, carnivals, funerals, football matches, housewarming parties and the Christmas market. Save yourself the alcohol! Save yourself embarrassing situations at the deposit bottle machine (which is common in Germany at least) or bottle banks. Save yourself embarrassing party photos or stories that suddenly start circulating on social media and in the office and save yourself evenings that you can no longer remember!

20 Get rid of dark circles

That makes you look pretty old: Yesterday you were partying like a lark and today you're scared of your own mirror image? "Here's looking at you, kid" really isn't necessary today! The blue, grey and red discolouration around your eyes is mainly caused by dehydration, lack of sleep and excessive alcohol consumption. Your skin lacks oxygen in the blood and alcohol also flushes important salts and minerals out of the body. In the long term, skin tissue and cell structure also suffer as a result. Of course, you can refill your vitamin and mineral levels with an appropriate diet (go for fruit and vegetables), but the best way to get rid of those annoying dark circles under your eyes is to stay away from alcohol in future and next time you drink water or a tasty fruit cocktail (alcohol-free, of course). Dark circles are not only caused by nights out. Perhaps you are simply stressed and overworked and therefore have trouble sleeping. Having a glass of red wine can help in the short term, but then you can forget about getting a good night's sleep. You can find better ideas in the section "Get a good night´s sleep".

21 Improve your skin

You've actually been out of puberty for a long time but your facial skin still sometimes looks like a teenager's? You've tried everything - from expensive face lotions to creams, medication and saunas - but nothing helps? Then why not try giving up alcohol? Alcohol is known as a true beauty killer and has a negative effect on your skin. Because the alcohol molecule passes through almost all pores, it confuses your hormone balance and moisture levels, stimulates the production of sebum and even makes you sweat more quickly.

Regular consumption of alcohol weakens the immune system - resulting in inflammation and redness (of the skin). Don't do this to your skin! Forget expensive scrubs and facial cleansers and skip the alcohol more often.

Extratip

There are also numerous apps that can help you to better control or manage your alcohol consumption: from drinking diaries, health coaching and alcohol calculators to drinking trackers. There is, for example, the "Sober grid" app, which is more of a social network where like-minded people can network and exchange information anonymously. Incidentally, it is no surprise that people like to use new technologies for these very sensitive topics because they can remain anonymous and try out what works best for them.

22 Do your body a favour

Did you know that in the European Middle Ages, beer was almost the only source of drink and even replaced entire meals for some people? The term "Dark Ages" should rather refer to dark beer.

In those days, water was undrinkable, so (beer) hops became the most important source of drink and food. Therefore, if you want to save a few calories today, you should stay away from alcohol. It has a lot of calories. Even small portions cover half of your daily requirement of energy. Here is a small example (per 100 ml): Wine spritzer has 34 kcal, wheat beer has 37 kcal, dry white wine has 69 kcal and sparkling wine climbs up to 76 kcal. The highest values are found in the well-known party drinks alcopops with 100 kcal, caipirinha with 144 kcal and mai tai with 180 kcal. Schnapps tops the list with 213 kcal and Pina Colada climbs to a record level with 240 kcal per 100 ml. So it's no wonder that alcohol is also known to make you fat. And as if that wasn't enough, it also stops the metabolism of fat and causes cravings, which in turn are satisfied at the nearest fast food restaurant. What a crazy idea, don't you think?

23 Go on a fast

At the beginning of this guide you have already tried it: a week without alcohol. How did you get on? Why don't you try such a drinking fast more often in future, it would do you good.

As a Christian term, the Germanic word "fast" comes from the Old High German word fastēn, which originates from the verb "to hold fast". In this context, you can ask yourself how firm or confident you are. Can you resist the temptations of everyday life and say "no" when you need to? Fasting periods are a great opportunity to find out and practise this in particular. Occasional or long-term abstinence has its advantages: you make a conscious and voluntary decision to take a break. This relieves your body and mind. You discover new sides to yourself. You explore your potential and limits. "How far can I go? And what am I capable of? "You also explore your special relationship with alcohol. The fasting period is a time for reflection. Perhaps you use it to refocus, do more sport or change your lifestyle. Decide for yourself how long you want your individual fast to last, when you want to start it and how you want to "break" it. Breaking your fast can actually be also a challenge. Your body will most likely react sensitively to the first alcoholic drink, which you should see as an advantage. After a few sips of wine or beer, you will probably realise how little you can tolerate. And don't reward yourself with alcohol for your supposedly strong stamina. Otherwise this will lead to false neuronal connections (alcohol as a reward = positive).

We drink alcohol not only to relax or to make the evening more enjoyable, but often also when and because we are stressed. Unfortunately, stress cannot be avoided in everyday life. Stress is not just the domain of work, nor is it a phenomenon of the modern age; it affects us all at all times and in all places. Our ancestors in the Stone Age usually reacted to stress with fight or flight! But what can we do today? For many people today, the easiest thing to do is to drown their anger, sorrow and frustration in alcohol. This may seem plausible as an emergency solution! Simply forgetting everything and quickly taking your mind off things - I'm sure everyone has done that at some point. But it doesn't help much in the long run. It is better to learn to deal with the problem and the associated negative feelings as well as possible in good time. In addition to the mindfulness-based method (see also the section "Meditating against the urge to drink"), we can achieve this wonderfully with progressive muscle relaxation. For example, with the "Becker fist" (actually made famous by the former German tennis player Boris Becker). Stress reduction with the clenched fist is based on progressive muscle relaxation according to Jacobson. Here, a shift in tension is achieved through concentration and transfer to the clenched fist. By opening the fist, the whole body relaxes at the same time. This method can be used in all critical situations when the pressure becomes too great again.

25 Becoming a tea sommelier

What is the "sensory specialty" of a Dornfelder or Riesling? Is the wine full-bodied, balanced or astringent? What is its surface tension like, does it form "tears" and how does the good wine behave in the aftertaste?

Have you always wondered what these so-called connoisseurs are actually talking about? If you really want to become an expert in a field, then try becoming a tea sommelier with really exciting stories: Tea culture has a tradition at least as long and interesting as that of wine. The beginnings are estimated to date back to 3000 BC, and a tea tax was levied relatively early on in the motherland of China. Tea appeals to all the senses. It is good for your health and can be drunk in company or alone. Its preparation is as varied as the types and flavors that exist. Enjoy your favorite cup of tea and learn more about its origin, cultivation and production in the various regions (e.g. Sri Lanka, China or Kenya). Take a trip around the world and get to know different cultures, rituals and ceremonies: Tibetan butter tea, the traditional British way of tea time or

Japanese-style sado. In Russia, it comes from the samovar, in Turkey, it's the two-part Çaydanlik. And did you know that the East Frisians are among the world's drinking champions with around 300 liters per head per year? As you can see, as a tea drinker you are about to go on an exciting journey of discovery.

26 Get a good night's sleep

Actually, you might think that a glass in the evening would calm your nerves and lull you straight to sleep. Not so! The supposed nightcap actually causes poor sleep. Although we are immediately tired after a few glasses of alcohol, but we can forget about deep sleep. The body cannot regenerate properly during the night because it is busy eliminating the alcohol from the body as quickly as possible. Waking phases because you urgently need to go to the toilet and feel very thirsty at the same time also disrupt your sleep rhythm. Besides, are you already looking forward to the night-time snoring? The alcohol-induced narrowing of the windpipe makes you an unpleasant musician. Your partner (and your neighbors) will definitely not be happy with such whistling dissonances. So it's better to keep your hands off the glass in the evening and use natural sleep aids instead. Some people prefer a short walk in the fresh air, others read a boring book or drink a cup of soothing chamomile tea. Little changes in the room also help: dimmed lights, brief airing, a harder mattress, fresh bed linen and, if possible, a regular day-night rhythm. If you feel really comfortable in your feathers, nothing will keep you from a restful night.

Break habits

We automatically associate many situations with drinking - but why? It's better to try something else.

We've already talked about it: There are situations in which a glass of wine is simply a must. We've never questioned it before! But think about it now. If you want to relax a little, forget stress or lift your mood - instead of alcohol - why not do it with meditation or music instead? There are even more tricks. Let yourself be surprised by the following alcohol-free methods.

27 Change your habits

Everyone has that one or two unpleasant habits that we would like to finally get rid of. For example, the often-thoughtless use of alcohol. We almost regularly fall back on alcohol in the evening, at the weekend of course and at parties anyway! At the same time, it's really annoying that good intentions are simply forgotten in everyday life. How do we change that? Well, there's no one-size-fits-all solution. We can try taking our minds off things and focusing on other, new things. But when it comes to alcohol in particular, it's difficult because alcohol is omnipresent in our society.

We only learn new habits with a clear mind and regular repetition. But first we need to know exactly what we really want. We are often accompanied by destructive thought patterns, i.e. ideas and notions that stand in our way like stones. Phrases such as "It's because of my difficult childhood" or "It's always been like this, there's nothing we can do about it" don't get us anywhere, and yet we say them again and again. Such sentences and views narrow our vision, reinforce entrenched structures and become a trap, especially in stressful situations. However, we can only take responsibility for our thoughts and actions if we are completely and "dryly" with ourselves. We make the world the way we like it, right? And that has nothing to do with "drinking the world into shape". Sober initiative is required. This is the only way to finally switch from autopilot to autonomy and turn bad habits into good ones.

28 Use the power of music

Music gets under your skin and sounds create moods, as you know only too well when you think back to the last crime thriller, for example. It's hard to imagine life without music. Why don't you get into the habit of using the power of sound to calm yourself down, put you in a good mood and, of course, relieve stress? Singing instead of sipping and dancing instead of drinking. You've already started in the tip "Enjoy unforgettable evenings".

"But I'm so tone-deaf", are you thinking now? Not at all. Music is in all our bones and you come across it everywhere in nature. Get yourself in tune! Perhaps you would like to sing in a choir or play in a band? But it's also enough to simply warble along to your favorite song in the shower or in the car. Fill your body with sound instead of schnapps and let the music play.

Music therapists emphasise that just one hour of singing has a positive effect on the whole body: You move your jaw, stomach and lungs and positively influence your physical posture. You train your vocal confidence and stimulate blood circulation of course. At the same time, you reduce the stress hormone cortisol and strengthen your immune system. Making music together connects people and fosters communication - the same effect as alcohol, only much healthier.

29 Use glasses and bottles in a different way

What do you do with all those pretty wine glasses when you're drinking less alcohol or none at all? Don't worry, there are lots of creative ways to use them in a different way, for example as decoration: fill the pretty glasses with colourful pebbles, dried flowers or other decorative objects and place them on open shelves. This looks fantastic, especially in the dining room and kitchen! Not bad either: wine glasses are ideal for desserts such as pudding, parfait, ice cream or chocolate mousse. As the glasses are transparent, you can layer the various ingredients in the glass to create attractive dessert creations. After all, a feast for the eyes.

If you still have empty wine bottles in the house, you can use them as candlesticks, for example. Pointed candles or conical candles are particularly suitable for this! And of course you can also decorate wine glasses with tea lights. This creates an incredibly cosy atmosphere. And you can conjure up great lighting effects if you also fill the glasses with fine sand or stones. And remember that you can also give the wine glasses as gifts if you don't have any use for them anymore. Perhaps someone else will be delighted with the beautiful crockery.

Obviously, you can still drink from the glasses - you can pour yourself juices, lemonades, iced tea, smoothies or water with fresh fruit or herbs (you will find some alternative drinking ideas further on in this book).

30 Dance yourself into a trance

For many people, going dancing and drinking alcohol usually go hand in hand. That's a shame, because the dance floor is easiest to hit when you're sober and the rhythm will put you in a trance after a while - even without the help of alcohol! Swing your legs across the floor, even if it feels a little strange at the beginning and you might have to be a little braver. Slowly feel your way to the beat and feel the rhythm. If you belong to the group of people who have to work up the confidence to go dancing, practise alone in front of the mirror at home before you venture out to the nearest club. Dancing - like everything else - needs to be learnt. For inspiration, take a look at the cult films "Dirty Dancing", "Flashdance", "Fame" or "Footloose". Modern versions are for example "Step Up", "Honey", "Safe the last Dance" or "Black Swan". You should also take a look at dance choreographies on the internet. If your self-confidence doesn't always come right away, immerse yourself in the dancing crowd and just go with the flow. Missteps are hardly noticeable here. The only important thing is not to be confused, but to have fun. After all, there is no perfect move, only the wrong outfit. However, you are definitely won't leave the area sober so soon - without alcohol in your blood, you will last longer - and soon you will make a new name as Dancing Queen (or King)! If you discover a new talent in yourself, why not try a proper dance class?

Imagine starting your Monday morning in a great mood, motivated and well rested. You drive to work whistling happily and start the week in a cheerful mood. Sounds weard? Not at all, because you can change the way you start the week by making the most of your weekend instead of lounging around on the sofa with a hangover.

Allow yourself a really long weekend for activities, sport and relaxation. And of course, the best way to do this is to avoid alcohol as much as possible. Most people complain that their weekends are far too short. No wonder, when they basically only really use one day and have to sober up the rest of the time. Saturday night was fun, but then they spend Sunday sluggishly in their pyjamas on the couch, bored in front of the TV, and probably with a terrible headache and a nasty stomach ache.

So you can actually forget about Sunday completely - what a pity! If you had done without the extra beer the night before, you could finally get out of bed earlier today, do a long-planned sporting activity, prepare breakfast for your loved one and plan an action-packed day out. Instead, you're annoyed that it was so late again last night, you complain about feeling unwell and probably swear to yourself - and not for the first time - that you'll "never drink again!" Why don't you give up alcohol and finally enjoy a long weekend?

32 Draw on your inner strength

Many people abuse alcohol as a supposed source of inspiration. They hope that drinking will give them a real boost of creativity. This may sometimes work. After all, we know that alcohol helps to relax and has a stimulating effect. But in the long term, our mental state becomes addicted to alcohol and the dose has to be gradually increased. It is better not to rely on the effect of alcohol, but instead draw your creative ideas from within, from yourself. Your own source is known to be endless.

But where exactly do we look for it, where does it come from and how can we use it practically? You can tap into sources, for example, by consciously focussing your attention, inner calm and mental training. This has nothing to do with esotericism or psycho-tricks. Rather, think of it as a kind of refuelling station for your mind by taking enough time to relax and reflect, sort out your thoughts and listen deeply to yourself. With the help of certain techniques such as yoga, autogenic training or meditation, you can find the deep inner strength you need for the creative process. Above all, you need patience and peace of mind. Condition your thoughts to the desirable goal, give your subconscious the order, then the result will come soon. Just believe it. And above all: trust in yourself and your strengths.

33 Meditate against the desire for alcohol

Meditation is a proven method to reduce stress and everyday problems. It consists of a formal and an informal practice: on the one hand, you consciously withdraw from everyday life and take a few minutes of reflection and contemplation for yourself. You can do this regularly to establish a certain routine. The second form of meditation is fully integrated into everyday life: Conscious cooking, mindful dishwashing and constant concentration on the present moment. The meditative practice puts you in a kind of observer role. Neuronal brain scans confirm the effect: regular meditation provides lasting relief from stress, anxiety and personal problems. Find a healthy balance to everyday life and relax. Practise meditative contemplation by looking at yourself and the current scenario from a distance, analyse your thoughts and learn to consciously let go. Who or what is responsible for the stress, the discomfort, the difficult emotions? And as you gradually learn to defuse the situation without making judgements, you will automatically feel calm and relaxed. Alcohol will soon become obsolete if you relax. Use meditation to combat the lust to drink! When the next stressful or critical situation arises in which you would normally turn to alcohol for help, quickly find a cosy spot and simply meditate the problem away.

Extratip

MBSR was founded in the 1970s by the American doctor John Kabat Zinn and is a mindfulness practice based on Buddhism. Zinn developed an eight-week stress management programme focusing on meditation, communication, boundary experience and mindfulness with the aim of becoming more aware of oneself again, being in the here and now, exploring the causes of stress in oneself and discovering new perspectives. MBSR is an excellent method to combat the constant and perhaps sometimes problematic craving for alcohol.

34 Beware of new addictions

Certain addictions are often linked to the consumption of other substances. For example, abstaining from alcohol can also curb cigarette smoking, because one sometimes goes hand in hand with the other. However, abstinence from alcohol can, on the contrary, awaken another, new craving, sometimes even insidiously and unconsciously. For example, you suddenly find yourself constantly snacking, becoming a caffeine junkie or constantly reaching for a packet of cigarettes. Become aware of this fact and take timely action to counteract it. Many non-alcoholic drinks also turn out to be real sugar traps. You may save yourself a few calories by cutting out alcohol (tip: "Do something good for your body"), but you'll probably be adding a lot more sweet products to your shopping list. Candy sugar in your chai, syrup in your spritzer or sweet cream in your cocoa. To avoid stumbling from one addiction to another, it is important to pay close attention and replace sugary foods with a healthier alternative: If necessary, use xylitol or stevia to sweeten drinks and food. Dried dates can replace a slice of cake and fresh fruit and berries are completely sufficient as sweet ingredients in spritzers (you can find more helpful tips on sweet cravings in the book "Die 50 besten Zuckersucht-Killer", published by TRIAS).

35 Celebrities as role models

You are not alone in saying "no" to alcohol. Abstaining from alcohol is the trend: Jennifer Lopez, Drew Barrymore, Kate Moss, Naomi Campbell, Leona Lewis, Lana Del Rey, Lucy Hale, Katy Perry, Miley Cyrus, Christina Ricci, Kim Kardashian, Natalie Portman and Michelle Hunziker prefer to reach for a glass of water instead of a high-proof drink. This is not only "good for your look", but also ensures a slim line.

And the men's world also prefers to drink "mocktails" (a new word combination of "cocktail" and the term "to mock", which means "to imitate, pretend"). David Beckham, Jim

Carrey, Karl Lagerfeld († 2019), Liam Neeson, Colin Farrell and Daniel Radcliffe all steer clear of booze and cocktails.

Paradoxically, it's the stars and starlets who drink alcoholic beverages on the big screen: Bradley Cooper (from the film "Hangover"), Gerard Butler (we know him from "300"), Eva Mendes ("Fast & Furious") and Freddie Frinton (the drunken waiter from "Dinner for One"). You see, it's not that unusual to swap your champagne glass for a glass of fizzy water. You're already one of the trend-setters with your decision.

36 Ask the experts

Just a few years ago, the World Health Organisation (WHO) issued a recommendation on how many grams of alcohol a man or woman can safely consume. Today it distances itself from these recommendations! According to current knowledge (2023), "there is no amount that is harmless to health". This is a remarkable statement that has never been made before, and the WHO is probably absolutely right! Every 10 seconds, one person worldwide dies as a result of alcohol (especially in the 20 to 39 age group). According to the WHO, more than 13% of all deaths are linked to alcohol. Founded in 1948, the Geneva-based United Nations specialised agency for public health points out that it is not the beverage (be it vodka, champagne or wheat beer) which is the problem, but the alcohol itself. It is toxic, psychoactive and addictive. Alcohol is even said to be responsible for a number of cancers, and unfortunately the risk starts with the first few drops. Over the last few years, the tone with regard to our alcohol consumption has become much harsher. Where previously there was still talk of a possible safe level and alcohol was even said to have positive effects such as lowering LDL cholesterol, preventing thrombosis or increasing the insulin sensitivity of cells (and thus preventing adult-onset diabetes), today there is a clear backpedalling and even a warning! The WHO emphasises that there are no studies that prove the possible positive effects of alcohol. The stuff is neither good for the heart nor does it help against diabetes. Alcohol is a cytotoxin and even the smallest amounts are harmful to health.

Especially the liver suffers from alcohol consumption. The liver is our detox expert and its job is to break down the alcohol as quickly as possible. This is quite exhausting! It manages about 0.1 per mille per hour (it doesn't get any faster!). During this time, all other metabolic processes are paralysed. Good nutrients, e.g. from a tasty meal, are now stuck in a traffic jam. Our liver hates multitasking! It is well organised and doesn't like to be disturbed. After all, it bears great responsibility for our optimal supply of sugar, vitamins, fats and protein. So "don't let a louse run over your liver", as the Germans used to say: Don't keep annoying your liver with unnecessary detoxification work.

So if you need professional help or still have questions, you can turn to helplines in your city, for example. There are now many centres all over the world, especially online, which can be reached at any time. First points of contact are

- https://www.nhs.uk/ – NHS the biggest health website for England
- https://www.niaaa.nih.gov/ - National Institute on Alcohol Abuse and Alcoholism in the USA
- https://alcoholchange.org.uk/ - Alcohol Change UK a charity company
- https://www.drinkaware.co.uk/ - Drinkaware, an Alcohol support service in London, UK
- https://americanaddictioncenters.org/ - Amercian Addiction Center

Alcohol-free drinks

Whether non-alcoholic beer, wine or cocktails with zero alcohol - non-alcoholic drinks are available in all shapes and sizes - healthy and delicious.

No more excuses! There are so many great alternatives that you can simply swap for a glass of alcohol. Of course, every start is hard, especially if you've been used to nothing else for years. But try it anyway. Here are a few delicious drinks.

At first glance, alcohol (C_2H_5O) and water (H_2O) hardly seem to differ in their molecular composition. Both consist of the elements hydrogen (H) and oxygen (O). Both substances are clear and transparent and definitely have one thing in common: both water and alcohol are indispensable and ubiquitous in our society. But this is also where they part ways: we can do without alcohol completely, but water is essential for life! You quickly realise this when you suddenly feel thirsty. We consist of 70 percent water (our brain even 85 percent) and need around 2.5 litres of water throughout the day. We sweat out up to one litre of water a day, and even more in high temperatures or during physical exertion. Accordingly, we need to keep refuelling. Not in the form of beer or shandy, of course, but with water or tea. H_2O is our fuel, we need it to be able to think and function at all. So it's not surprising that water is celebrated as the "new wine".

So, which "fuel" would you prefer - classic, medium or still? Spring water or table water? Fluoride-containing or low-sodium? From the tap, from the bottle or directly from the spring?

38 Turn your home bar into a fruit oasis

If you're the proud owner of a chic home bar, why not plan your next party alcohol-free? Store the last drops of alcoholic drinks in the cellar and transform your bar into a real fruit oasis.

The eye "drinks" too: Fill the minibar with lemonade, water and fresh juices, for example, and decorate the counter like a beach bar in Hawaii. There are no limits when mixing: Serve the grape juice in a wine goblet and sip the freshly squeezed lime juice from a martini glass. But multi-coloured creations made from pineapple juice, coconut milk, apple sauce and soda are also fruity, fresh and delicious. The advantage of your newly equipped home bar: you can start drinking as soon as you get up in the morning without feeling guilty. Simply add your espresso machine from the kitchen and you'll make getting up twice as much fun.

39 Drinking green

Green, green, green ... are all my mixed drinks - and these are anything but alcoholic! Have you ever put salad and herbs in the blender? Show your colours and give it a try: Rocket, arugula, parsley, broccoli, spinach, kiwi, pumpkin, mint or salad leaves, plus a fresh green apple, lime, sugarsnap peas, pear or some pineapple juice.

Add 1/2 litre of water and blend the ingredients until you have a thick juice. Grapes, leek, aloe vera, honeydew melon or avocado are also green. Even if the flavour may take some getting used to, especially because of the bitter substances, green fruit and vegetables contain a lot of antioxidants and plenty of vitamin B. Not only is this a great alternative to alcohol, it's also really wonderful to look at (and serve). I promise your friends will be very impressed. They've never seen anything like it! Boost your health and your immune system. The green plants are also a source of iron and folic acid. So, are you already in the green zone?

40 Give milkshakes a try

If you say "no" to alcohol more often and - as the saying goes, "slide down my hump" - you can actually do something for your back instead: for example, do more sport and improve your fitness. Then you'll quickly get to know the athlete's favourite drink: Cool milkshakes - "shaken, not stirred", of course. James Bond, who is known to drink a lot during his investigations (up to 900 ml of pure alcohol in a week), would be jealous. This is because the high protein level in milkshakes really fills you up and provides great muscles. Simply pour 300 ml of milk (alternatively 250 g of natural yoghurt or a cup of buttermilk), a banana and some vanilla (ideally use real vanilla from the pod) into a glass. Blend everything together and just skip the sugar or replace it with an alternative sweetener! Add a dash of lemon or orange juice to lift the mood, coconut milk or passion fruit juice for a Caribbean flavour and coffee, guarana or cocoa for an energising effect. You can achieve the beautifully creamy result either with a suitable blender or with your new muscle power in a tightly sealed keep-fresh cup. Depending on the temperature outside, add crushed ice to the glass and go ahead, shake it!

41 Try non-alcoholic shots

The "nightcap" as a digestive schnapps has become commonplace, just like the aperitif before a meal. Herbal bitters, plum brandy or clear spirits are used to alleviate the unpleasant feeling of fullness after a sumptuous three-course meal. It is better to try a non-alcoholic alternative. The best thing to do after a big meal is to get moving again and go for a long walk. If you're feeling peckish after a big meal or are planning a party where aperitifs and shots cannot be missed, here are some tasty alternatives: "shots" (usually a 2 cl or 4 cl glass) made from sea buckthorn, lime or lemon juice. Also try blackberry, blackcurrant or unsweetened cranberry mother juice. Straight juices are a real pick-me-up because of their tangy, bitter flavour. And if you have stomach problems, a freshly cooked ginger tea may help. Peel the ginger, cut it into small pieces and pour hot water over it. The longer you brew the tea, the better the tuber works.

Extratip

We know the cranberry mainly from American films in which Thanksgiving is celebrated with plenty of cranberry sauce. However, the pink berry, the stamens of which resemble the beak of a crane, is also conquering our bakeries. Dried, it tastes a little bitter and is therefore a great alternative to the usual sultanas. It is also said to help with diarrhoea and prevent bladder and urinary problems. Why not raise a toast next time with an alcohol-free Pink Dream (made from soda water, cranberries and other red fruits) - very healthy and delicious.

42 Drink herbal tea instead of herbal schnapps

Now you know that schnapps is not really conducive to good digestion. In fact, the alcohol has a negative effect on the body. As an aperitif before a meal, it makes you more hungry because the sugar (glucose) in it raises your glucose levels and stimulates your appetite. Alcohol also paralyses the digestive muscles and delays the natural emptying of the stomach - so it's not a good choice to drink after a meal. If anything helps here, it's probably the herbs in the schnapps. But why not go straight to the herbal kitchen? After all, Traditional Chinese Medicine (TCM) has sworn by the healing properties of herbs for thousands of years: teas made from caraway, fennel or savoury ensure that your "Qi" (life force) flows throughout your body. Get your energy juices flowing with a blend of herbs that you put together, for example 40 g caraway seeds, 20 g coriander seeds, 20 g fennel seeds and 2 aniseed stars. Or you can simply choose the quick option in the form of pre-packed tea bags from the supermarket. Tea also plays an important role in Indian Ayurveda: Pitta tea has a balancing effect (= mint, jasmine, rose petals), Vata has a relaxing effect (= orange blossom, southernwood, cinnamon) and Kapha has a stimulating effect (= ginger, cloves, saffron).

And here are a few more tips from the healthy herb garden:

- Valerian is pure calming. Valerian tea is the best choice after a stressful day. It also helps with insomnia, nervousness and irritability.

- Lemon balm not only smells fresh, but also calms the nerves and reduces the desire for alcohol. Rubbing the leaves creates a pleasant fresh flavour. Now add a delicious lemon balm and blackcurrant drink - and the day is in the pot of gold.

- Only mint is truly refreshing. It not only refines every drink you make, but also has a healing effect on the stomach and intestines and keeps your head cool.

- Even the ancient Egyptians swore by the "flower of the sun" - camomile. It is also the most popular medicinal plant in this country and a real all-rounder: it is effective for inflammation of the mouth and throat, cramps, toothache and intestinal complaints.

- Sage, on the other hand, has a very intense flavour, but with a dash of honey/stevia in the tea, hoarseness, sore throats or problems with the sweat glands quickly disappear.

- And above all, fennel is a real hangover killer. It not only helps with digestion and sleep problems, but also relieves headaches, hoarseness and fatigue the morning after.

43 Refreshment from heaven

In the vast, tropical landscapes of Hawaii, where the majestic coconut palms seem to touch the sky, the repeated appearance of falling coconuts is a mesmerising spectacle. The scenes of coconuts seemingly sailing out of the blue sky vividly convey the idea of a place full of natural beauty and wonder. After all, how else would it get the unusual name "Noelani", which means "freshness from the sky". In Brazil, it is considered the national drink, but the coconut drink is gradually finding its way onto supermarket shelves here too.

Coconut water is the fruit water of a young (still green) coconut and the trendy drink par excellence (not to be confused with the fatty and viscous coconut milk, which is obtained from the flesh of a ripe, i.e. brown coconut). The coconut drink has only 16 calories (per 100 g), little sugar from the fruit, but plenty of minerals.

As a refreshing and electrolyte drink, coconut water not only fascinates athletes, but is also a great party drink to show off. The coconut drink (for around €2) is now available in practical drink packs and in all major supermarkets, organic food shops, health food shops and chemists. The heavenly drink tastes particularly good chilled with a straw from a martini glass.

44 Drink a "little wet one"

The world-famous and traditional long drink from Cuba has probably tickled the palates of many people. You will certainly have tried it long ago. The meaning of the name "mojito" as "the little wet one" refers to the very unusual origin of the term, which is derived from the word "mojar" and means "to get wet". It was first mentioned in the 16th century and has been attributed a certain magical allure ever since.

The drink's unmistakable potency, which comes from the invigorating freshness of the lime and the unmistakable flavour of the dried mint leaves, has certainly impressed personalities such as Ernest Hemingway (1899-1961). Its flavour exudes a refreshing aura that invigorates the senses and enlightens the mind, which is almost certainly due to the fresh mint. Why not create your own 'little wet one' by mixing carbonated soda water with 2.5cl of freshly squeezed lime juice and adding 6-8 fragrant mint leaves, 2 teaspoons of cane sugar (or optionally xylitol or stevia) and a handful of ice cubes. You can buy the green mint leaves at various markets, in Turkish or Moroccan grocery shops or in tea houses. Incidentally, there are over 600 different varieties of mint, many of which can even grow easily in your own garden or in a simple flower pot on a sunny balcony.

If you grow your own mint, you will always have it to hand when you feel like having a little refreshment. Believe me, this drink will make summer your favourite season.

45 How about cocktails for a clear head?

The sparkling cocktail from South Tyrol called "Hugo" has also arrived in Germany since 2010 at the latest. It is above all its pink colour, which is created by the juice of elderflower (or alternatively lemon balm), that inspires us. But where does this name come from? Pure coincidence, at least according to the inventor. Originally, however, Hugo is an old Germanic masculine first name that actually stands for "mind" and "thinking spirit". What a funny coincidence, don't you think? The interesting thing is that Hugo later evolved into Hubert, Hauke and Hugh.

The ingredients elderberry and lemon balm are indeed stimulating (but only these): The elderberry is known in this country as the lilac berry bush and flowers mainly in early summer. Because of its high vitamin C concentration, the flowers and berries are often made up into juice, syrup, tea or jam. Its flowers help with many complaints such as fever, insomnia, pain, skin problems and tiredness. Lemon balm, on the other hand, is known to calm the nerves, help with gastrointestinal problems and improve concentration. Even in the Middle Ages, people knew about its special healing powers and it belonged in every monastery garden. So if you need inspiration or a clear head, how about a homemade punch of strawberry and elderberry or tea with lemon balm and peppermint?

46 Cool down

Keep cool and quench your thirst with a mix of juices, bite-sized pieces of fruit and cooled teas. For example, use 100% fruit juices and mix them with spiced tea (chai), ginger tea, fruit tea or green tea. The caffeinated South American mate tea is also very popular. This mineral-rich slimming drink can be drunk hot or cold and flavoured with milk or lemon. Spices such as cinnamon, vanilla or chilli go well with chai. After brewing, leave the tea to infuse for a few minutes and allow to cooldown. You can then add some juice to it. It's best to make a whole pot so that you can drink it several times and don't have to make a new tea every time.

And if you want to add fruit juice, don't use Necktar (it usually has added invert sugar, which you don't have to - it's better to use the 100% fruit variety). Mother juice is particularly productive. This is the juice obtained directly after the first pressing. Direct juices are filtered naturally, without the addition of additives, sugar, flavourings or artificial vitamins. Due to their high fruit content, they can be easily diluted with water and also taste natural and authentic. For a quick fix: Mineral water, a little juice, a piece of fruit and some mint (preferably from a tea bag) and you have the ultimate cool-down for hot summer days.

47 Warm up

Most people associate the Advent and Christmas season primarily with mulled wine, punch, grog and so-called Feuerzangenbowle. These hot drinks do not necessarily have to be alcoholic. After all, boiling the drinks makes them warm anyway. Alcohol as a " source of heat" is therefore unnecessary. Why not create your own naturally alcohol-free mulled wine this year with very simple ingredients? Briefly heat grape or blackcurrant juice with ½ litre of water and a few slices of citrus fruit (grapefruit, orange, lime, lemon or mandarin) in a pot. Season with a few peppercorns, chilli flakes, star anise, cinnamon, cardamom and cloves. Leave the mixture to infuse for around 10 minutes and your X-Mas drink is ready. And when Santa Claus makes his long journey to us, why don't you ask him to bring you some fresh wild berries for your hot drink (alternatively, you can use the frozen variety). This will make the winter time a little more cosy, right? These fruity, spicy creations have several benefits: they warm you up from the inside, they are vitamin bombs, help to burn fat and give extra energy. This is perfect for combating the winter blues, when there is no sun anyway and we move less and go outside rarely at this time of year. Try other melting favourites too: Hot chocolate (made from 100% cocoa, mixed with hot water, a little low-fat milk and flavoured with cinnamon), spicy teas or invigorating coffees. Vanilla, ginger, nutmeg, honey, chilli, berries or a dollop of sugar-free, low-fat cream go particularly well with it.

Best hangover tips

Even good intentions can sometimes fail. Here are a few tricks for when you've tried to do too much and it hasn't worked out.

As you already know, the liver needs a few hours to break down the alcohol. In the meantime, you can "hang over" the line and sleep off your drunkenness in peace.

48 Hang over the line

Well, did it get a little late again yesterday and did you drink a little more than you intended? At least that's what some of the symptoms suggest. As good as the party was yesterday, the morning after is anything but intoxicating. What stupidity! Your head is buzzing, your stomach is tightening and those dark circles under your eyes!

The term "hangover" probably comes from the Victorian era in England. At that time, there were supposedly rooms in the capital, London, where homeless people could sleep or rest on a tightly stretched rope for two pennies a night. They hung over this rope and sometimes slept off their drunkenness.

In medical terms, "hangover" is known as "veisalgia", with the typical symptoms of malaise, headaches, loss of appetite and impaired performance. Trace elements, salts and minerals are "flushed out" of the body by the alcohol. This loss leads to headaches and aching limbs.

So the first thing you need to do is balance your mineral levels and get fit again. Eat a good breakfast, drink enough (for example, a vegetable broth, which provides you with everything you need right now) and get a good night's sleep. Then you will quickly recover your strength and no longer have to „hang over" the ropes.

Extratip

To get rid of the hangover as quickly as possible, there are some absurd suggestions. Listen to this:

- Number 3: Go to the sauna to simply sweat out the residual alcohol.
- Number 2: Simply fast for a while and get rid of all those calories from last night.
- 1st place: Counteract this with a counter beer, following the homeopathic principle of "fighting like with like".

Just keep your hands off it! You will already know what you need now - starvation, sweating and afterglow certainly not.

49 Banish the hangover

Get your circulation going again. A strong coffee is just the beginning. The body tries to break down the alcohol quickly. Your liver has a lot of work to do. You will feel this more or less painfully all over your body. Support the process from the outside: drink plenty of water, have a good breakfast with plenty of vitamin C (ideally from lemon or orange juice).

And then take a Kneipp cure (yes, you heard that right): Kneipp has nothing to do with the German word "Kneipe" (pub), but with "Kneipp", the inventor of the cold-hot therapy. Alternating showers are a great way to get rid of all that limpness. Start at your feet and slowly work your way up with the cold water jet. Can you already feel the refreshing kick? When you feel fit again, get out into the fresh air, lace up your running shoes and go for a leisurely jog. Just 20 minutes of light jogging or brisk walking will get your circulation going. If you already have a hangover, go for it and do something for your health.

Anyone who can "take a good boot" (as we say in German) is particularly hard-drinking. Have you heard that one too? Nothing to be proud of! It's just an indication that you have to drink more to feel the same effect as in the past. Too bad about all the money you have to spend now too. If we're already talking about "boots" and "cats" (hangover actually means "cat" in German), then we'd better take a look at "Puss in Boots" (fairytale character by Ludwig Tieck 1797).

Do you know the story? After the miller died and his goods and chattels were divided among his three sons, the youngest "only" got the tomcat. But what should you do with a tomcat? "Don't be so eager, we'll make the best of it," promised the small but smart little fellow. He just asked for a pair of nice boots and then went off to mingle with the people. With his wonderfully exhilarating nature and his funny, positive attitude to life, the self-confident cat finally caught the king's attention and helped the boy to wealth and prestige, all because he showed bravery and patience, but above all made the best of the situation.

So what have we learnt? Two things: You have also embarked on a new path. Perhaps you want to reduce your alcohol consumption or give it up completely. Great, lace up your new boots, which figuratively stand for courage, openness and a good dose of self-confidence. You don't need any liquid aids to help you go your own way. These will only cause you to slip. Be optimistic and relaxed. After all, only the cat has "nine lives". But you only have this one! Make the best of it! I wish you as much success as many other readers of this book!

Alcohol test

Check yourself: are you in control or is your consumption already critical?

Question	Yes	No
I drink alcohol several times a week.	❑	❑
It's often more than two glasses.	❑	❑
I also drink high-proof spirits.	❑	❑
I can tolerate quite a bit of alcohol.	❑	❑
I can drink a lot of alcohol. People have noticed that.	❑	❑
There are times when I just get drunk without reason.	❑	❑
I can't imagine a weekend without alcohol.	❑	❑
I often feel guilty about my consumption.	❑	❑
I wanted to stop drinking alcohol once.	❑	❑
The family has always been good at drinking.	❑	❑
Drink driving has unfortunately also happened to me.	❑	❑
Occasionally I have a film break after a party.	❑	❑
When I'm drinking, I'm also quick to argue.	❑	❑
Objects sometimes fly [because of this].	❑	❑

When I drink, my emotions are often confused. ❏ ❏

I had my first sip of alcohol quite early on. ❏ ❏

My consumption has increased over the years. ❏ ❏

A little beer belly is already noticeable. ❏ ❏

Alcohol is often my favourite quick consolation. ❏ ❏

I need alcohol for stimulation. ❏ ❏

Sometimes I drink alone (secretly). ❏ ❏

I've injured myself before while I was drunk. ❏ ❏

Well, where have you ticked your boxes? If the "yes" outweighs the "no", then it's high time to go alcohol-free!